An

EMPTY TOMB

and a

GARDEN OF

RISEN HOPE

✳

There came a rich man from Arimathea named Joseph, who had himself become a disciple of Jesus. Going to Pilate, he asked for Jesus' body and Pilate ordered that it be given to him. Joseph took the body, wrapped it in a clean linen cloth and placed it in his own new tomb that he had cut out of the rock.

Matthew 27,57-59 (NIV)

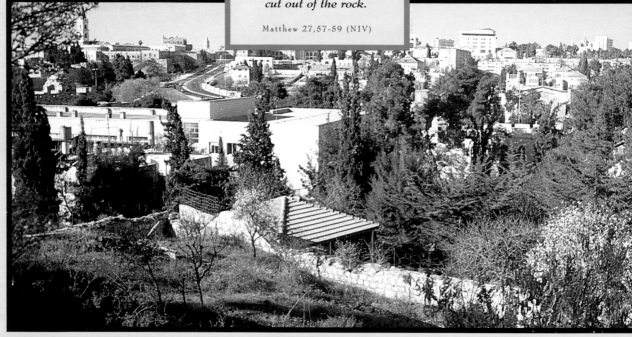

View of Garden from the cemetery wall.

Similar view taken in 1896

Two thousand years ago a rocky outcrop by a busy thoroughfare skirting the city of Jerusalem was a good place for a burial chamber. Many believe this may have been the site of the tomb which Joseph of Arimathea, a secret follower of the Lord Jesus Christ, gave for his burial after the crucifixion. Archaeologists suggest that the Garden Tomb may have been cut in the first century AD, the period when Christ ministered on earth. Today the site is a beautiful and peaceful garden, shielded by buildings and a steep escarpment from the noisy and vigorous city all around. And the empty tomb is a reminder of a risen, living Saviour in a harsh, uncaring world.

Thousands of visitors from across the world visit this special place every year. Many are 'surprised by joy' as they discover a clearer understanding of Christ's ministry, death and resurrection. Bible narratives come to life, bringing peace and new hope.

On the following pages we seek to recapture those scenes and thoughts as we walk through the Resurrection Garden to the empty Tomb.

CONTENTS

In building the temple, only blocks dressed at the quarry were used, and no hammer, chisel or any other tool was heard at the temple site while it was being built.

1 Kings 6,7 (NIV)

There is much to be seen from the Garden's viewing platform. The 16c city walls are impressive, high and impregnable on a rock bluff. That limestone outcrop is part of Mount Moriah, which runs through the old city to Temple Mount where the Dome of the Rock now stands.

When Solomon started building his temple there around 950 BC, he took stone from this northern site - and workings under the wall are still known as Solomon's Quarry. It left a vast open space, ideal for traders to gather with their caravans of camels and donkeys or, in recent years, fleets of buses! But the area near Skull Hill also acquired another name: Beit-ha-Sekilah... the Place of Stoning, a place for executions.

Christ was crucified somewhere close to Jerusalem, but no one knows the exact site. Quintillian, a Roman writer, says they always crucified criminals by crowded highways to warn as many as possible. And this busy space by the roads to Jericho and Damascus is an appropriate spot.

Left: The Damascus Gate

Below: City Walls

Above right: Skull Hill

Many separate verses in the Bible paint a scene for the crucifixion that is remarkably like the area of Skull Hill and the Garden. It was outside the city gate *(Hebrews 13, 12)* and near the city *(John 19, 20)*. People passed by, insulting Christ on the cross *(Matthew 27, 39)* while friends stood at a distance *(Luke 23,49)*.

There is no hint in Scripture of a green hilltop, but of a noisy open site by a busy road. Oddly, it was called the Place of the Skull (Aramaic: Golgotha; Latin: Calvary, a bald place). And overlooking this 'bald' former-quarry by busy roads there still remains a cliff, crumbled into shapes like a skull...

They came to a place called Golgotha, which means 'The Place of the Skull'. There they offered Jesus wine mixed with a bitter substance; but after tasting it, he would not drink it. They crucified him and then divided his clothes among them by throwing dice.

Matthew 27, 33
(GNB)

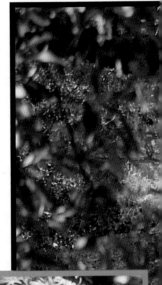

All over the Roman Empire criminals were executed by nailing to a post or cross - it was a public and prolonged way to die. Yet Christ's death was different... Although Jesus had broken no Roman law, Pontius Pilate succumbed to Jewish demands for the death penalty to punish 'blasphemy'. But most important of all, Jesus Christ went willingly and deliberately to his own death, having told his followers that this would happen and why: to give eternal life to those who believed in him (John 3,15); to give his own life as a ransom for many others (Matthew 20, 28); to overcome Satan's power (John 12, 31); to allow sins to be forgiven (Luke 24, 47). Without Jesus' death, there would be an impassable barrier between God and sinful men and women.

For Christ died for
sins once for all, the
righteous for the
unrighteous, to bring
you to God.

1 Peter 3, 18 (NIV)

Because so much of the New Testament account of Jesus' final hours on earth can be visualised in the Garden, its quietness and peace give opportunity for reflection; an opportunity to consider what the Bible says about it all.

The climax of the Bible account is not the wooden cross or the briefly-used tomb, but the resurrection of Jesus Christ. The most important fact about the tomb is that it is empty, and that Jesus really did rise from the dead and is alive. We too can therefore be sure that a new life also awaits us, his followers, when we die.

> *But Christ has indeed been raised from the dead, the firstfruits of those who have fallen asleep. For since death came through a man, the resurrection of the dead comes also through a man. For as in Adam all die, so in Christ all will be made alive.*
>
> 1 Corinthians 15, 20-22
> (NIV)

Photo: Garo Nalbandian

The Lord will guide you always; he will satisfy your needs in a sun-scorched land and will strengthen your frame. You will be like a well-watered garden, like a spring whose waters never fail.

Isaiah 58, 11 (NIV)

It is easy to see that this place has long been a garden - and possibly was the one mentioned in John's Gospel where Joseph of Arimathea had prepared his family tomb prior to Jesus' death. Water is essential in the long, hot Jerusalem summer, so water cisterns were dug to collect the winter rains. Here there are several - one of them is the third largest in the city. There is also a wine press, suggesting a vineyard. So when a deep layer of earth and rubble was removed from apparently derelict land in the 1890s, it was possible to restore the site as a garden.

Left: Inside the large cistern, of pre-Christian origin

Above and right: Winepress

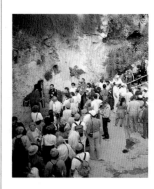

The cross on the inside walls indicates later Christian use of Tomb

Apart from historical and geographical circumstances, there is much in the Gospels to commend the Garden Tomb as the place where Jesus' body was laid after the crucifixion. It is not a natural cave but is hewn out of solid rock; the tomb appears to be unfinished; it has a groove in front for a rolling stone to close up the entrance (inevitably, that useful stone has not remained here for 2000 years); from outside you can see (as a disciple did) the recess for the body; and it is large enough for several people to go inside (as the women and the apostle Peter did).

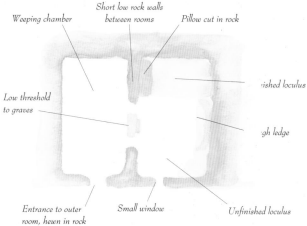

Weeping chamber

Short low rock walls between rooms

Pillow cut in rock

Low threshold to graves

...ished loculus

...gh ledge

Entrance to outer room, hewn in rock

Small window

Unfinished loculus

PLAN OF THE TOMB

As evening approached, there came a rich man from Arimathea named Joseph, who had himself become a disciple of Jesus. Going to Pilate, he asked for Jesus' body and Pilate ordered that it be given to him. Joseph took the body, wrapped it in a clean linen cloth and placed it in his own new tomb that he had cut out of the rock. He rolled a big stone in front of the entrance to the tomb and went away.

Matthew 27, 57-60 (NIV)

In a place like this, Mary Magdala, dustraught with grief and despair, through her tears mistook the risen Jesus for the gardener. Then Jesus called her name - and she knew the truth. The Garden is still today a place where tears can be wiped away and uncertainties about Jesus can lead on to the discovery of his reality.

Left: A rolling stone - but much smaller than the original

Early on the first day of the week Mary Magdalene went to the tomb and saw that the stone had been removed...

She turned round and saw Jesus standing there, but she did not realise that it was Jesus. Thinking he was the gardener, she said 'Sir, if you have carried him away, tell me where you have put him and I will get him.' Jesus said to her, 'Mary'...

Mary Magdalene went to the disciples with the news: 'I have seen the Lord"

John 20, parts (NIV)

God has raised
this very Jesus from
death, and we are all
witnesses to this fact.

Acts 3, 32 (GNB)

Debate about which site is correct has rumbled on for years, although there is no irrefutable proof at any location after so many centuries. Here, near the entrance to the Tomb, there are signs of an early Christian meeting place.

Yet how much does it matter? The Gospel writers only touch lightly on the whereabouts of the tomb, emphasising that the empty tomb meant Christ was risen - and alive.

The apostle Paul makes no mention of the tomb when teaching the certainty of the physical resurrection of the Saviour. Clearly our faith in the risen Jesus does not depend on knowing where he was buried or seeing the site.

We know from the testimonies of the first believers and from our own experience of his presence today that he lives. It is the person who matters, not the place - as it says on the door of the Garden Tomb: 'He is not here; for He is risen.'

The Lord Jesus, on the night he was betrayed, took bread, and when he had given thanks, he broke it and said, 'This is my body, which is for you; do this in remembrance of me.' In the same way, after supper he took the cup, saying, 'This cup is the new covenant in my blood; do this, whenever you drink it, in remembrance of me.' For whenever you eat this bread and drink this cup, you proclaim the Lord's death until he comes.

1 Corinthians 11, 23-26(NIV)

The Last Supper, just before the death of Christ, was significant in many ways - the Passover meal recalled centuries of God's mercy and what Jesus said held promise of an even greater mercy to come. Today as an act of commitment and worship, that simple meal is regularly relived by visitors to the Resurrection Garden. Sitting in its leafy shade, a whole world of people can be found praying and worshipping in many languages as they take the bread and the wine...

Easter Day is a very special day in the Resurrection Garden. Worshipping with the empty tomb as a visual aid helps us to re-live the experience of Mary, John and the others when their despair and sadness on the day of crucifixion changed into joy and hope three days later. Every Easter Sunday hundreds come to the Garden, starting before dawn for successive services in six different languages until mid-day. They sing with fresh meaning Easter hymns such as 'Jesus Christ is risen today, hallelujah!'

In addition, on every Sunday throughout the year there is a 9am service to which people from all over the world find their way. Many people discover a new reality for their faith in Jesus as they worship him in 'this special place'.

For God so loved
the world that he
gave his one and
only Son, that
whoever believes in
him shall not perish
but have eternal life.

John 3, 16 (NIV)

Israel was part of the Turkish empire when, in 1867, a Greek man who owned some rough wasteland near Skull Hill, dug down into the rubble hoping to find a cistern. He discovered a hole in the rock, full of skulls and bones, but when an archaeologist told him that it was an ancient burial place the hole was abandoned.

It was some 16 years later that the celebrated British soldier and Bible student, General Gordon, looking from a friend's house on the city wall, was impressed by the topography of the area and the skull-like appearance of the rock. He realised that this could be the site of Golgotha.

Much later (indeed, after Gordon's murder in Khartoum) interested Christians in Britain appealed through The Times newspaper of 22nd September 1892 for £2000 to buy and maintain the tomb and land around it. The Garden Tomb Association was founded the next year and in 1894, the tomb and garden was purchased from the then German owners - 'that it might be kept sacred as a quiet spot'. Since then on this site the Association has been proclaiming the very heart of the Christian faith, the dying and living of the Lord Jesus Christ.

Background picture: The old city of Jerusalem, 1883

Right: The earliest known picture of the Garden Tomb before complete excavations took place

Top right: Jeremiah's Grotto, 1870

Top left: Skull Hill and Garden site from City walls

Below right: Ariel view, taken around 1947

> The Lord is our God; his commands are for all the world. He will keep his covenant for ever, his promises for a thousand generations.
>
> Psalm 105, 7-8 (GNB)

> *Praise be to the God and Father of our Lord Jesus Christ! In his great mercy he has given us new birth into a living hope through the resurrection of Jesus Christ from the dead, and into an inheritance that can never perish, spoil or fade.*
>
> 1 Peter 1, 3 (NIV)

There were strong objections from Ottoman officialdom to the purchase of the site, but the British and German consuls added their influence. Eventually the sale was agreed on condition that a strong wall was built to separate the area from the old, unfenced Muslim cemetery on the hill.

Over the intervening years the Garden has attracted more and more visitors, and staffing and facilities have increased to cope. Volunteer guides and shop staff live on site for short periods, working with the Jerusalem team. Of the thousands of visitors who come throughout the year, many regard their visit to the Garden as the spiritual high point of their time in Israel. They love the sacredness of this quiet spot, as lives are changed and faith is renewed.

On the door into the Garden Tomb is a verse from the Bible that touches the heart of Christ's Gospel: He is not here, for He is risen...

It tells why a death by cruel torture that took place nearly 2000 years ago has and will have a lasting effect on the relationship between human beings and God. Jesus literally died for us - in our place he accepted the anger and the punishment of God for our sin. Those who believe can know the risen Lord in a living and personal way. That is the message of the empty tomb... alleluia!

HE IS NOT HERE,
FOR HE IS RISEN.
ALLELUIA!

Since we have confidence to enter the Most Holy Place by the blood of Jesus, by a new and living way opened for us... let us draw near to God with a sincere heart in full assurance of faith.

Hebrews 10, 19-22
(NIV)